Pink Stars and Angel Wings

Story by
SUSAN EKBERG

Illustrated by
MICHELLE NEAVILL

Spiritseeker Publishing, Inc., Fargo, ND

Library of Congress Cataloging-in-Publication Data
Ekberg, Susan, 1960 —
    Pink stars and angel wings / by Susan Ekberg;
illustrated by Michelle Neavill.
        p. cm.
    Summary: A little girl discovers that she has a guardian angel.
    ISBN 0-9630419-0-8 : $16.95
    [1. Angels–Fiction.]   I. Neavill, Michelle, ill. II. Title.
PZ7.E3473P1   1992
[E]–dc20   91-91216

Typeset and Printed by Richtman's Printing and Packaging, Fargo, ND

This Book belongs to:_____

To Mom and Dad (who've always believed in me), to Kari and Erik (my two little angels), and to H.C. (my earthly guardian angel) — I love you all.

— S.E.

To my family & Jim with love.

— M.N.

Kari loved stars. She loved how they twinkled. She loved how they stayed up in the sky. And she loved the story her mother told her, about her special star.

"When you were born, God gave you your own star. There are many stars in the sky, but the one that makes your tummy flip-flop, the one that almost seems to talk to you, that's your special star.

"But you have to look for it, and you must believe it is waiting for you."

1-2-3-4 . . . every night Kari counted them. "But there are *so* many children in the world". . . 5-6-7 . . . "What if there aren't enough stars? What if there isn't one for me?" . . . 8-9-10 . . . "I want to go see it — I wonder what's there?"

One night Kari looked up, and there, right at the end of the Big Dipper's handle, was a star she hadn't seen before.

It was a beautiful, sparkling pink star, a
tummy flip-flopping, talking-kind-of-star.

She fairly flew into the house.

"Mommy,
I saw it — MY star,
and it's PINK — do you
think it's really mine?"

"You know the story, Kari," her mother said.
"When you go to sleep tonight, tell your
secret wish to the star."

Kari could hardly wait. Jump, jump into her
nightie . . . brush, brush her teeth . . . "Thank you
God for stars, and God bless everybody in the
world" . . . hop, hop under her cozy comforter.

"Good night, sweet one," her mother whispered
in her ear.

Kari closed her eyes, and the "I-remembers" of the day swirled slowly by, then faded, faded, to fuzzy-edged dreams . . .

"I wish I could go see you, pink star," Kari whispered.

Wish, whoosh, Kari swooshed through the window, her
long brown braid a kite's tail behind her, the leaves of
the giant elm tree tickling her toes as she breezed by.

Looking up, there it was —
the star — *her* star, and she heard
it say, "Come, Kari, come."

It was fun to be like a bird,
twirling and somersaulting,
stars streaking by, wind
kissing her ears.

Closer and closer, the pink star
became a pink cloud,

and Kari bounced on it

three times

before she sank through its cotton candy fluff.

POOOOF! Kari landed.

She stood up, swatted pink dust off her nightie, and looked around. "Just like the pictures I paint, where the colors are all mixed up!"

Floating, floating toward her — a pink cloud!!

Kari giggled, and rubbed her eyes. She saw a rainbow above the cloud, like a beautiful fan, a rainbow peacock fan.

The cloud became a woman, her face
so light that Kari had to cover her eyes.

For a second.

Kari's mother *had told* her about angels.

"Welcome, little Kari. I'm happy you're here." Musical words, floating words, angel words.

"How do you know me?" asked Kari.

"I've always known you, Kari, from the very beginning. I'm your guardian angel. I'm always with you, protecting you, guarding you, loving you.

"Do you remember when you fell off your bed? I was the one who caught you. And remember the nights when you were scared of the monsters that hunched in your closet? I was the one who held you and rocked you until you fell asleep."

"Yes, YES, I remember, but I've never *seen* you. Do you hide?"

"You don't see me with your eyes, Kari. I'm the voice you hear when the rest of your world is quiet."

"Yes, I've heard you. I call you Kate. That's your name. Kate. My uncle Pete says you're not real, that you're im-a-gi-nary, but I don't believe him. Kate, where *are* we? Is this heaven? Is it really real?"

"Listen to your heart, Kari. What does it tell you?"

"It tells me this is like heaven, but it's not. It's where I go when I dream. Someone is always with me, and I feel so happy, like I'm being hugged from the inside out, and it's so warm.

"I try to tell people about my dreams, but they just look away."

"There are many things you'll learn, Kari. People need love in their hearts, or they can't hear the love that's in your heart."

"I'll *keep* telling them about love."

"*Tell them about the colors . . .*"

"I'll tell them about my star!"

"Tell them they can find theirs, too . . ."

Kari stood up, but kept her head bent.

"I know I have to go back, Kate, but will I ever see you again?" Kari looked up into deep blue eyes, so like her own.

"I have to stay here, Kari, but I'll always be with you. When you close your eyes and open your heart, I will be there," said the angel, patting Kari's nightgown over her heart.

"When you look in people's eyes, you will see me. And when your mother strokes your head, you will feel me.

"Love is all around you, just look . . ."

Kari looked at her right shoulder. A puffy little pink cloud was resting there.

Kari laughed, then ran into the angel's arms. So happy to feel
her warm, feathery wings surround her, so soft, so white, so . . .

Kari opened her eyes. Back in her room, her arms wrapped around her comforter.

Then she saw it on her pillow —

One perfect white feather,
wrapped in soft pink light.

"Remember, little Kari, I am with you always . . ."

"I love you, Kate."

A smile, a sigh, peaceful sleep.

Dear Friends:

When I was a little girl I spent my days talking to rocks, listening to the trees, "visiting" stars, and listening to the beautiful stories that my mother and father would tell me. It was a magical time, and one, that until recently, I thought was gone forever. But the magic came back when I started listening to my own children; how they each have imaginary playmates that they share their days with, how important their dreams are, and how everything in their lives is so *real,* so magical. As I opened myself up to that world again, *Pink Stars* was given to me, because that's all I can call it, as I opened my mouth one night and there it was.

My description of Kate was influenced by what John saw in his revelation (Rev. 10:1). I *do* believe in angels, and believe in much more than my eyes can see. I value the writings of the Tao te Ching, Kahlil Gibran, and the Native Americans because they all carry the message of universal love and self-understanding that is so needed for the mending of a broken world and people. I feel that message weaving through the ages, across the continents, from people's hearts to people's minds.

It is my hope that you will gain an understanding of *Pink Stars* that goes beyond its written words, talking to your children and others about what *they* believe. And it is my eternal hope that you all find your special star.

"You don't see me with your eyes, Kari. I'm the voice you hear when the rest of your world is quiet . . ."

—Kate